AF199042

Impressum
Verlag: BABADADA GmbH, Nedderfeld 112 , 22529 Hamburg
Geschäftsführer / Verlagsleitung: Harald Hof
Druck: Books on Demand GmbH, In de Tarpen 42, 22848 Norderstedt

Imprint
Publisher: BABADADA GmbH, Nedderfeld 112 , 22529 Hamburg, Germany
Managing Director / Publishing direction: Harald Hof
Print: Books on Demand GmbH, In de Tarpen 42, 22848 Norderstedt

school
School

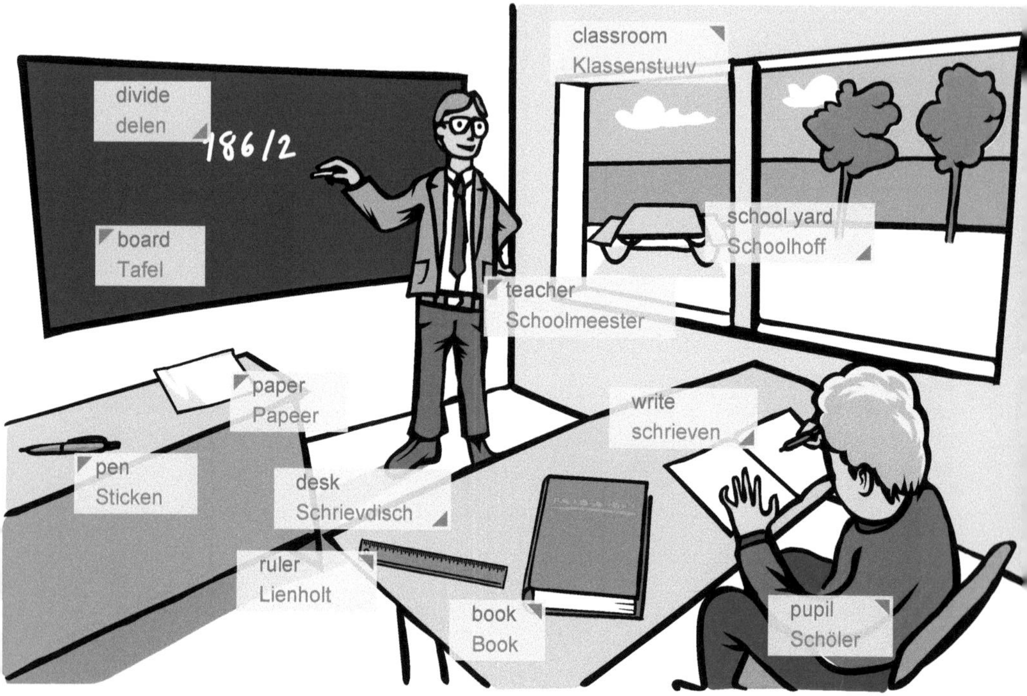
classroom
Klassenstuuv
divide
delen
186/2
board
Tafel
school yard
Schoolhoff
teacher
Schoolmeester
paper
Papeer
write
schrieven
pen
Sticken
desk
Schrievdisch
ruler
Lienholt
book
Book
pupil
Schöler

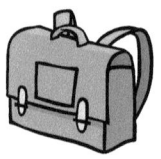

satchel
Ranzel

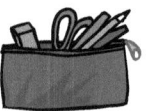

pencil case
Feddermapp

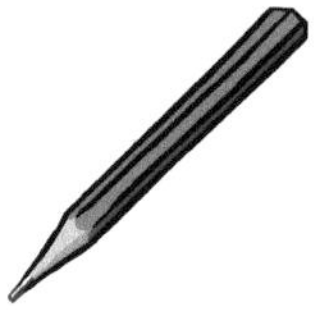

pencil
Bleesticken

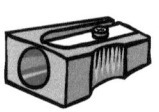

pencil sharpener
Scharpmaker

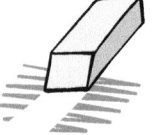

rubber
Radeergummi

drawing pad
Tekenblock

drawing

Teken

paintbrush

Pinsel

paint box

Malkassen

scissors

Scheer

glue

Klever

exercise book

Heft to'n Öven

homework

Huusopgaav

number

Tall

add

tohooptellen

subtract

aftrecken

multiply

malnehmen

calculate

reken

letter

Bookstaav

alphabet

ABC

word

Woort

text

Text

read

lesen

chalk

Kried

lesson

Stunn

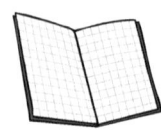

register

Klassenbook

examination

Pröven

certificate

Tüügnis

school uniform

Schooluniform

education

Utbillen

encyclopedia

Nakieksel

university

Universität

microscope

Mikroskop

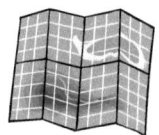

map

Koort

waste-paper basket

Papeerkorf

travel
Törn

hotel
Hotel
Grand
hostel
Harbarg
ROOMS
currency exchange office
Wesselstuuv
EXCHANGE
car
Auto

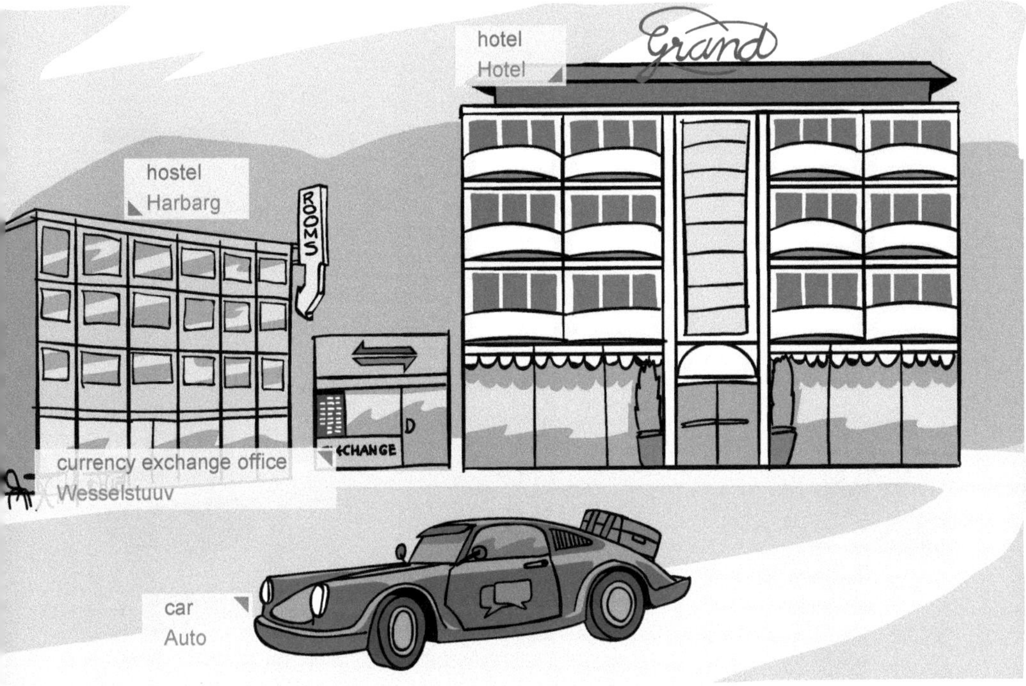

language

Spraak

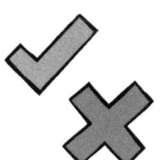

yes / no

jo / ne

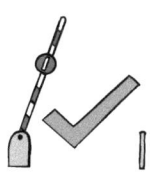

Okay

Jo

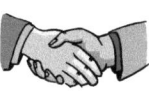

hello

Moin

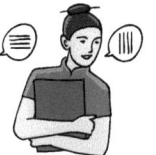

translator

Översetter

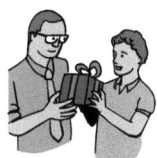

Thank you

Dank ok

how much is...?

Wat kost...?

I don´t get it

Ik verstah nich

problem

Problem

Good evening!

Goden Avend

Good morning!

Moin!

Good night!

Gode Nacht!

goodbye

Tschüüs

direction

Richt

luggage

Bagaasch

bag

Tasch

backpack

Rüchsack

guest

Gast

room

Stuuv

sleeping bag

Slaapsack

tent

Telt

tourist information
....
Touristeninformatschoon

beach
....
Strand

credit card
....
Kreditkoort

breakfast
....
Fröhstück

lunch
....
Meddageten

dinner
....
Avendeten

Ticket
....
Fohrkort

elevator
....
Fohrstohl

stamp
....
Breefmark

border
....
Grenz

customs
....
Toll

embassy
....
Bottschop

visa
....
Visum

passport
....
Pass

transport
Transport

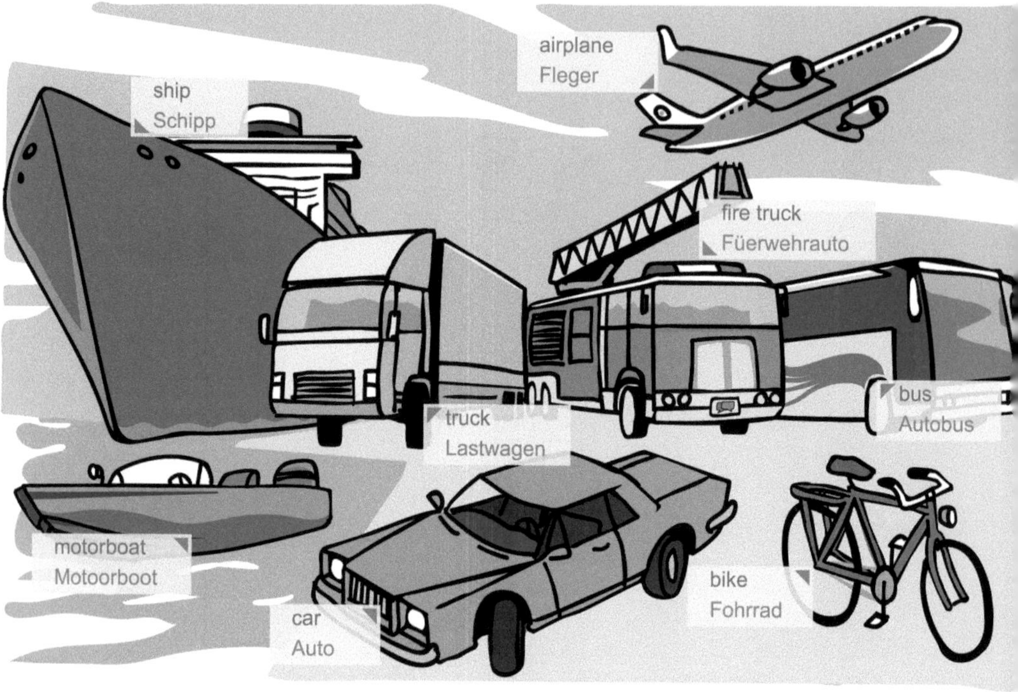

airplane
Fleger
ship
Schipp
fire truck
Füerwehrauto
truck
Lastwagen
bus
Autobus
motorboat
Motoorboot
bike
Fohrrad
car
Auto

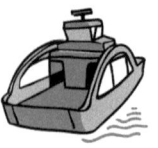

ferry

Fähr

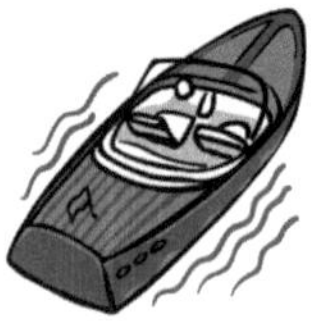

boat

Boot

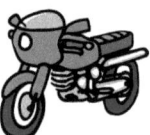

motorbike

Motoorrad

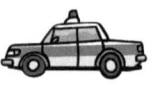

police car

Polizeiauto

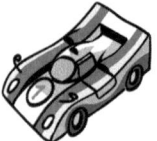

racing car

Rönnauto

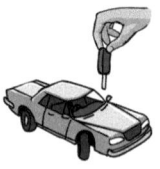

rental car

Lehnwagen

car sharing

Carsharing

tow truck

Afsleepwagen

garbage truck

Müllauto

engine

Motoor

fuel

Kraftstoff

fuel station

Tanksteed

traffic sign

Verkehrsschild

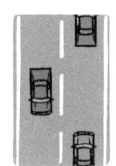

traffic

Verkehr

traffic jam

Stau

parking lot

Afstellplatz

train station

Bahnhoff

tracks

Sporen

train

Tog

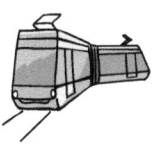

tram

Stratenbahn

wagon

Wagon

helicopter
Dwarsmöhl

airport
Flooghaven

tower
Tower

passenger
Fohrgast

container
Grootkist

carton
Karton

cart
Koor

basket
Korf

take off / land
starten / lannen

city

Stadt

village
Dörp

city center
Binnenstadt

house
Huus

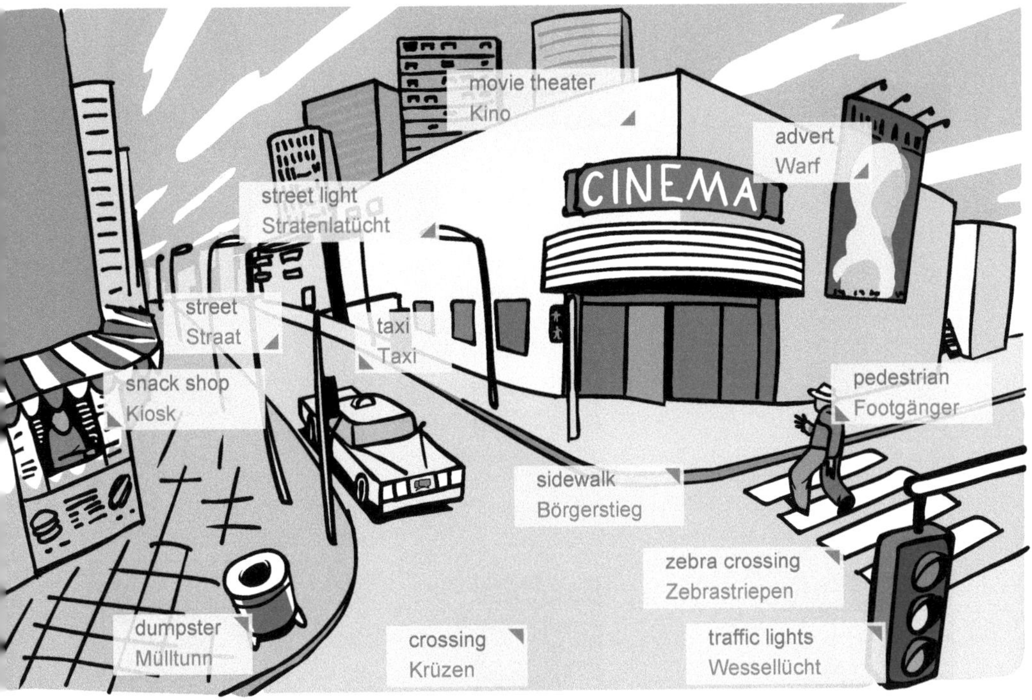

movie theater
Kino

advert
Warf

street light
Stratenlatücht

CINEMA

street
Straat

taxi
Taxi

snack shop
Kiosk

pedestrian
Footgänger

sidewalk
Börgerstieg

zebra crossing
Zebrastriepen

dumpster
Mülltunn

crossing
Krüzen

traffic lights
Wessellücht

hut

Hütt

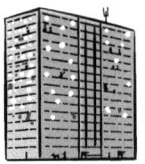

apartment

Wahnung

train station

Bahnhoff

city hall

Raathuus

museum

Museum

school

School

university

Universität

bank

Bank

hospital

Krankenhuus

hotel

Hotel

pharmacy

Afteek

office

Büro

book shop

Bookhökerie

shop

Hökerie

flower shop

Blomenhökerie

supermarket

Supermarkt

market

Markt

department store

Koophuus

fishmonger's shop

Fischhökerie

mall

Inkoopszentrum

harbor

Haven

park

Parkanlaag

bench

Bank

bridge

Brüch

stairs

Trepp

subway

Ünnergrundbahn

tunnel

Tunnel

bus stop

Busstoppsteed

bar

Bar

restaurant

Spieslokal

postbox

Breefkassen

street sign

Stratenschild

parking meter

Parkklock

zoo

Deertenpark

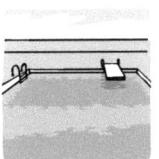

swimming pool

Baadanstalt

mosque

Moschee

farm

Buernhoff

pollution

Ümweltversmudden

cemetery

Karkhoff

church

Kark

playground

Speelplatz

temple

Tempel

landscape
Landschop

signpost
Wiespahl

path
Weg

meadow
Wisch

stone
Steen

hiker
Wannerer

tree
Boom

river
Fluss

grass
Gras

flower
Bloom

valley

Daal

hill

Barg

lake

See

forest

Holt

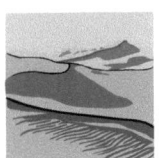

desert

Wööst

volcano

Füerspien Barg

castle

Slott

rainbow

Regenbagen

mushroom

Poggenstohl

palm tree

Palm

mosquito

Steekmück

fly

Fleeg

ant

Miegeemk

bee

Imm

spider

Spinn

beetle

Sebber

frog

Pogg

squirrel

Katteker

hedgehog

Swienegel

hare

Haas

owl

Uul

bird

Vagel

swan

Swaan

boar

Wildswien

deer

Hirsch

moose

Elk

dam

Staudamm

wind turbine

Windrad

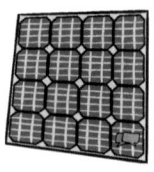

solar panel

Solarmodul

climate

Klima

restaurant
Spieslokal

waiter
Kellner
menu
Spieskoort
chair
Stohl
soup
Supp
pizza
Pizza
cutlery
Bestick
tablecloth
Dischdeek

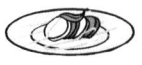

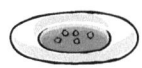

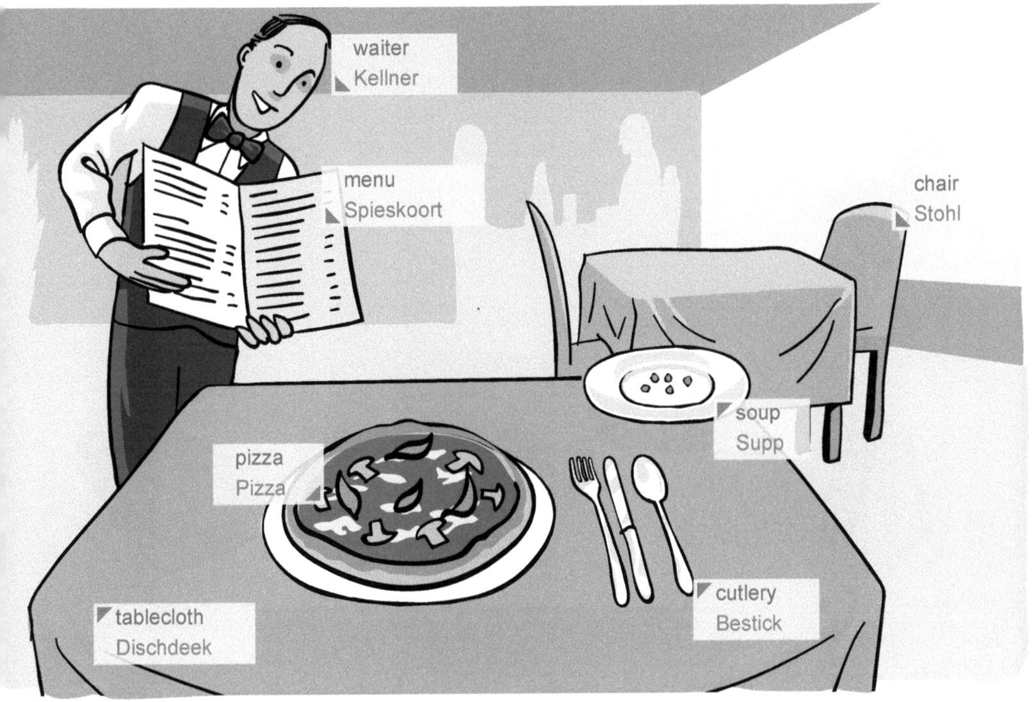

starter
Vörspies

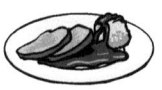

main course
Haupteten

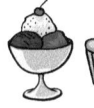

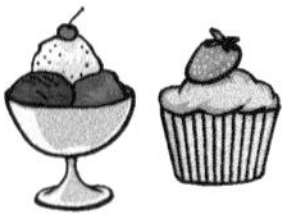

dessert
Nadisch

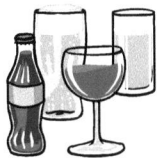

drinks
Drünk

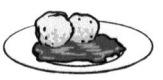

food
Eten

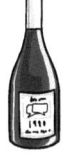

bottle
Buddel

fast food

Fastfood

street food

Strateneten

teapot

Teekann

sugar bowl

Zuckerdoos

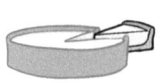

portion

Portschoon

espresso machine

Espressomaschien

high chair

Hoochstohl

bill

Reken

tray

Tablett

knife

Mess

fork

Gavel

spoon

Lepel

teaspoon

Teelepel

serviette

Munddook

glass

Glas

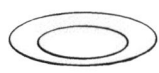

plate

Töller

soup plate

Suppentöller

saucer

Ünnertass

sauce

Sooß

salt shaker

Soltstreuer

pepper mill

Pepermöhl

vinegar

Etig

oil

Ööl

spices

Krüder

ketchup

Ketchup

mustard

Mostrich

mayonnaise

Mayonnaise

supermarket
Supermarkt

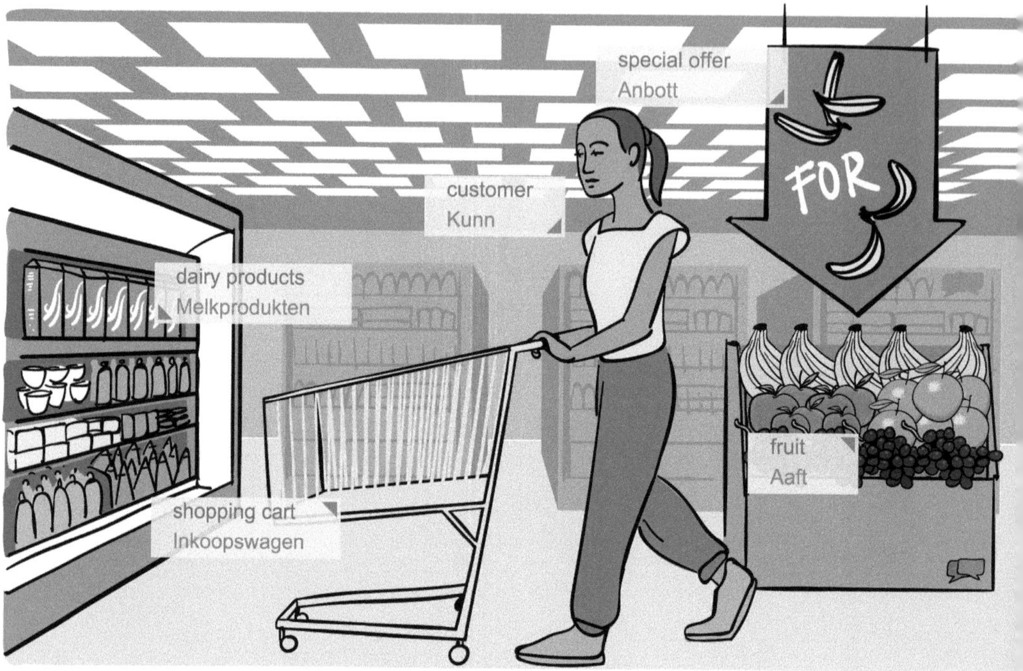

special offer
Anbott
FOR
customer
Kunn
dairy products
Melkprodukten
fruit
Aaft
shopping cart
Inkoopswagen

BUTCHERS

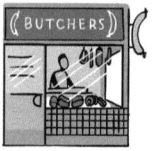

butcher's shop

Slachterie

BAKERY

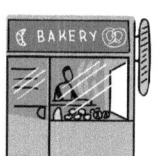

bakery

Bäckerie

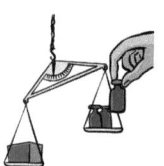

weigh

wegen

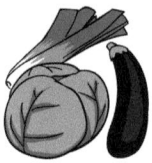

vegetables

Gröönsaken

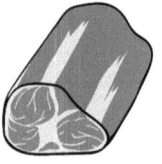

meat

Fleesch

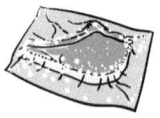

frozen food

Deepköhlkost

cold cuts

Opsnitt

canned food

Konserven

detergent

Waschmiddel

candy

Snoopkraam

household products

Huushooltssaken

cleaning products

Reinmaaktüüch

sales representative

Verköpersche

cash register

Kass

cashier

Kasserer

shopping list

Inkoopslist

opening hours

Opsparrtieden

wallet

Breeftasch

credit card

Kreditkoort

bag

Tasch

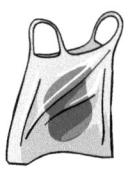

plastic bag

Plastiktüüt

water

Water

juice

Saft

milk

Melk

coke

Cola

wine

Wien

beer

Beer

alcohol

Spriet

cocoa

Kakao

tea

Tee

coffee

Koffie

espresso

Espresso

cappuccino

Cappucino

banana

Banaan

apple

Appel

orange

Appelsien

melon

Meloon

lemon

Zitroon

carrot

Wöttel

garlic

Knuuvlook

bamboo

Bambus

onion

Zibbel

mushroom

Poggenstohl

nuts

Nööt

noodles

Nudeln

spaghetti

Spaghetti

rice

Ries

salad

Salat

fries

Pommes frites

fried potatoes

Braadkantüffeln

pizza

Pizza

hamburger

Hamborger

sandwich

Sandwich

escalope

Snitzel

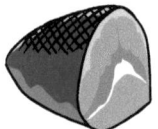

ham

Schinken

salami

Salami

sausage

Wust

chicken

Hohn

roast

Braden

fish

Fisch

porridge oats

Haverflocken

muesli

Müsli

cornflakes

Cornflakes

flour

Mehl

croissant

Croissant

bread roll

Rundstück

bread

Broot

toast

Toast

cookies

Keksen

butter

Botter

curd

Quark

cake

Koken

egg

Ei

fried egg

Spegelei

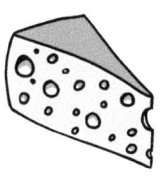

cheese

Kees

ice cream

les

sugar

Zucker

honey

Honnig

jelly

Marmelaad

nougat cream

Nougat-Creme

curry

Curry

farm
Buernhoff

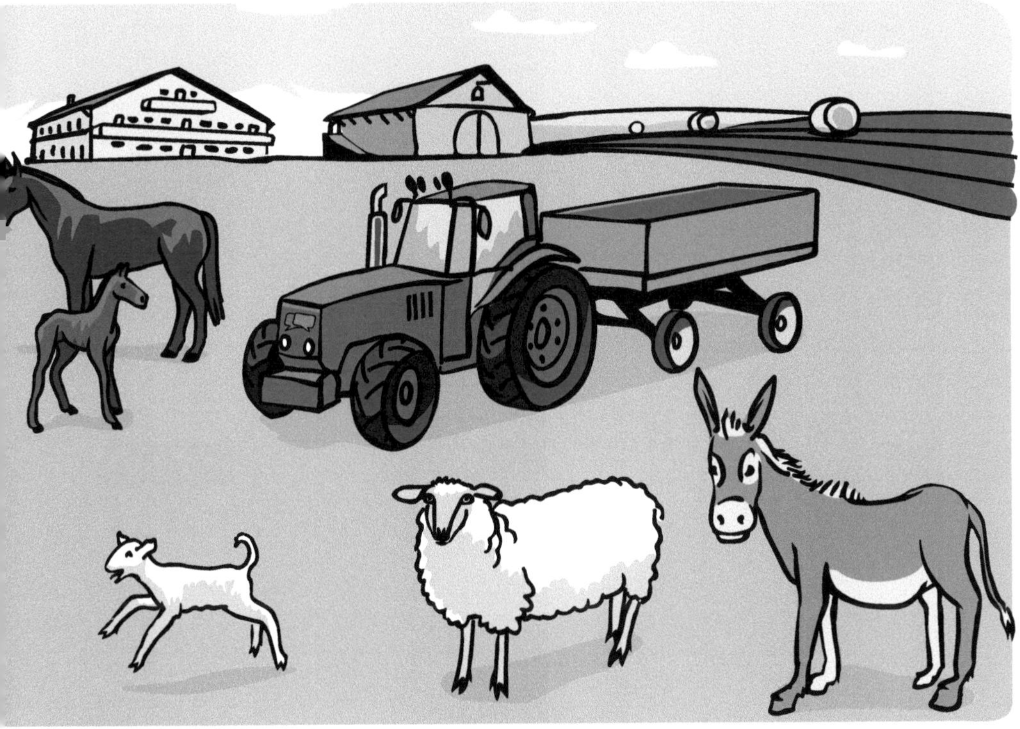

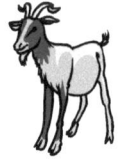

goat

Zeeg

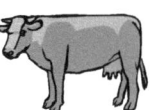

cow

Koh

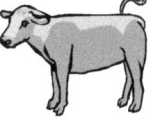

calf

Kalf

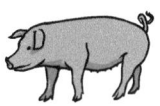

pig

Swien

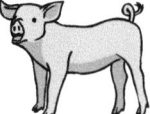

piglet

Farken

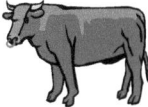

bull

Bull

goose

Goos

duck

Aant

chick

Küken

hen

Hohn

cockerel

Hahn

rat

Rott

cat

Katt

mouse

Muus

ox

Oss

dog

Hund

dog house

Hunnenhütt

garden hose

Goornslauch

watering can

Geetkann

scythe

Lee

plow

Ploog

sickle

Sich

hoe

Hack

pitchfork

Mestfork

axe

Ext

pushcart

Schuufkoor

trough

Trog

milk can

Melkkann

sack

Sack

fence

Tuun

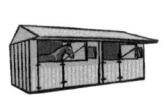

stable

Stall

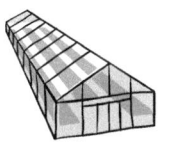

greenhouse

Drievhuus

soil

Bodden

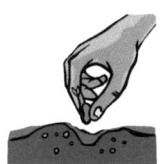

seed

Saat

fertilizer

Dünger

combine harvester

Meihdöscher

harvest

oornen

harvest

Oorn

yams

Yamswöttel

wheat

Weten

soya

Soja

potato

Kantüffel

corn

Törksche Weten

rapeseed

Rapp

fruit tree

Aaftboom

manioc

Troopsch Kantüffel

grain

Koorn

farm - Buernhoff

house
Huus

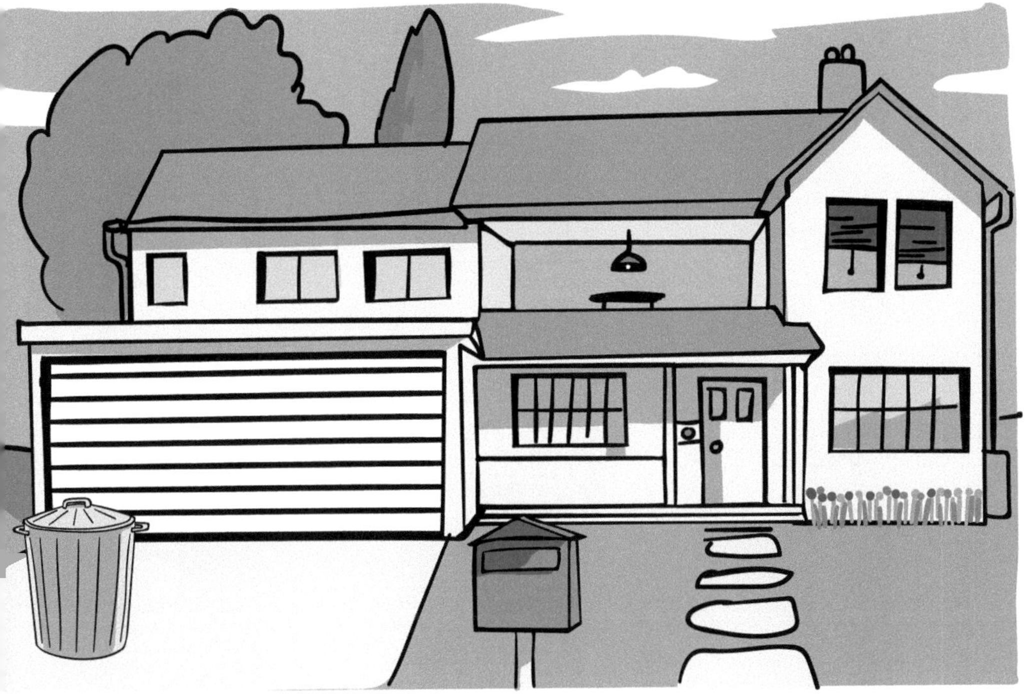

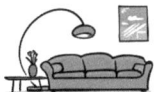

living room
Wahnstuuv

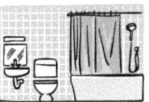

bathroom
Baadstuuv

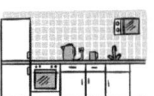

kitchen
Köök

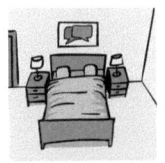

bedroom
Slaapstuuv

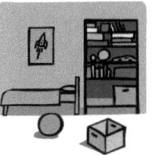

kids room
Kinnerstuuv

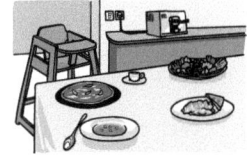

dining room
Eetstuuv

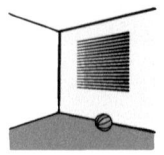

floor

Footbodden

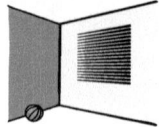

wall

Wand

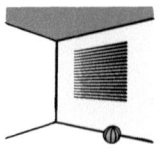

ceiling

Deek

cellar

Keller

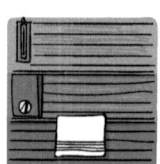

sauna

Hittluftbad

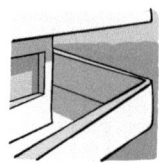

balcony

Balkon

terrace

Terrass

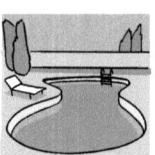

pool

Swümmbad

lawn mower

Rasenmeiher

sheet

Bettbetog

bedspread

Bettdeek

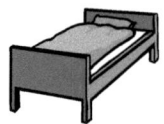

bed

Puuch

broom

Bessen

bucket

Emmer

switch

Schalter

living room
Wahnstuuv

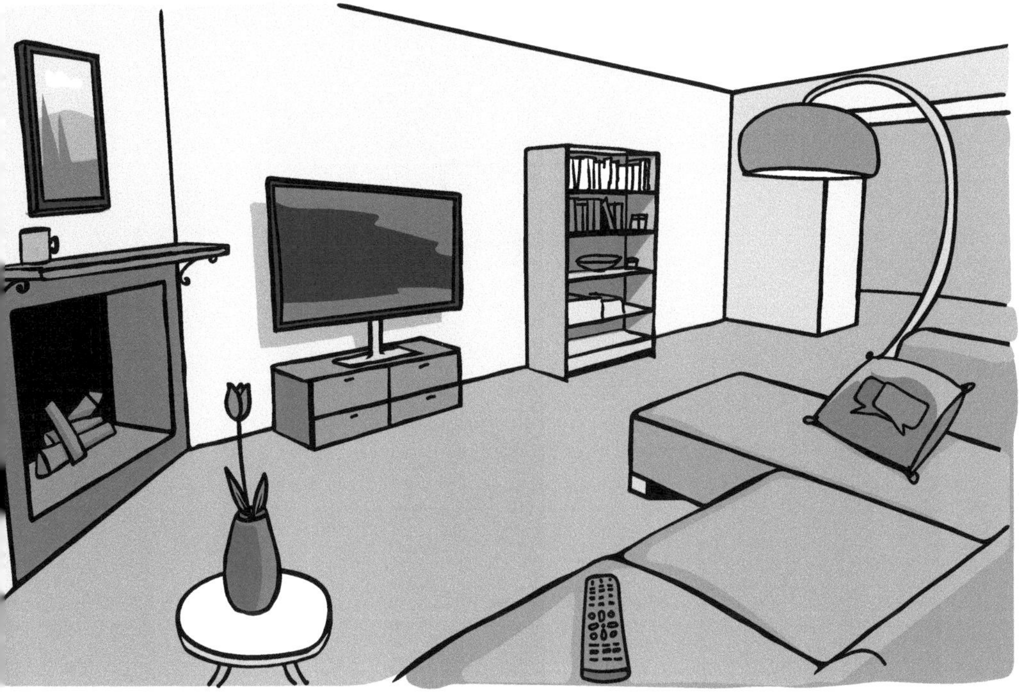

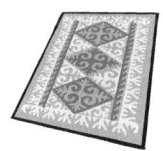

carpet
Teppich

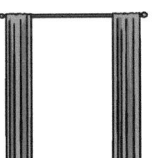

drape
Vörhang

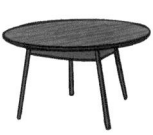

table
Disch

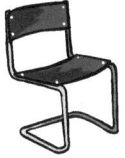

chair
Stohl

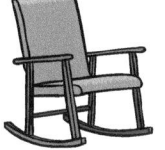

rocking chair
Schuckelstohl

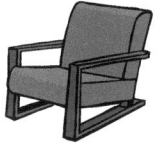

armchair
Sessel

book

Book

blanket

Deek

decoration

Dekoratschoon

firewood

Füerholt

film

Film

stereo system

Stereoanlaag

key

Slötel

newspaper

Narichtenblatt

painting

Gemälde

poster

Poster

radio

Radio

notebook

Opschrievblock

vacuum cleaner

Huulbessen

cactus

Kaktus

candle

Kars

kitchen
Köök

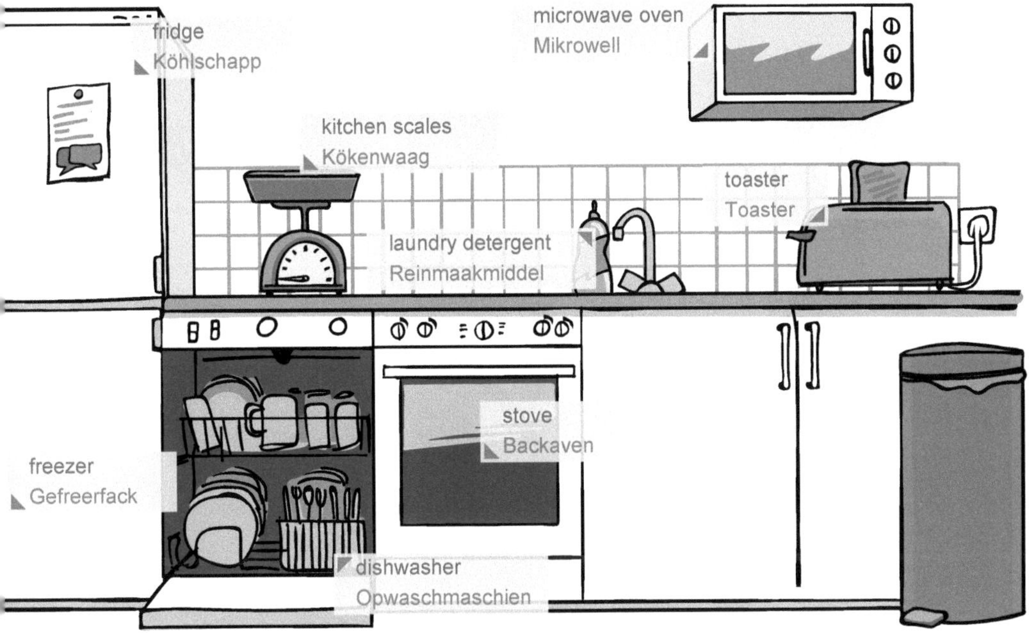
fridge
Köhlschapp
microwave oven
Mikrowell
kitchen scales
Kökenwaag
toaster
Toaster
laundry detergent
Reinmaakmiddel
stove
Backaven
freezer
Gefreerfack
dishwasher
Opwaschmaschien

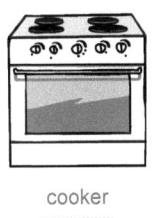

cooker

Heerd

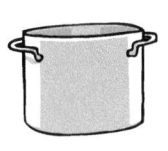

pot

Pott

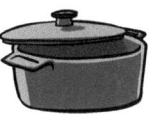

cast-iron pot

Gussiesern Putt

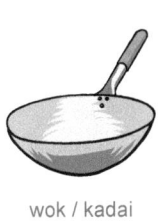

wok / kadai

Wok / Kadai

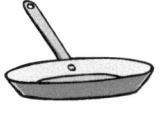

pan

Pann

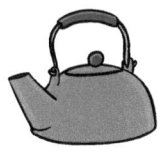

kettle

Waterkaker

steamer

Dampkaakputt

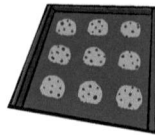

baking tray

Backblick

crockery

Geschirr

mug

Beker

bowl

Schaal

chopsticks

Eetsticken

ladle

Suppenkell

spatula

Pannenwenner

whisk

Sneebessen

strainer

Kaakseef

sieve

Seef

grater

Riev

mortar

Mörser

barbecue

Grill

fireplace

Füerstell

kitchen - Köök

chopping board
Sniedbrett

rolling pin
Nudelholt

corkscrew
Proppentrecker

can
Doos

can opener
Dosenaapner

oven cloth
Pottlappen

sink
Waschbecken

brush
Böst

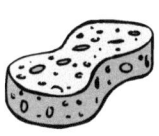

sponge
Swamm

blender
Mixer

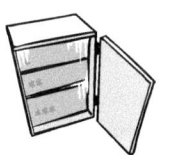

deep freezer
lesschapp

baby bottle
Nuckelbuddel

tap
Waterhahn

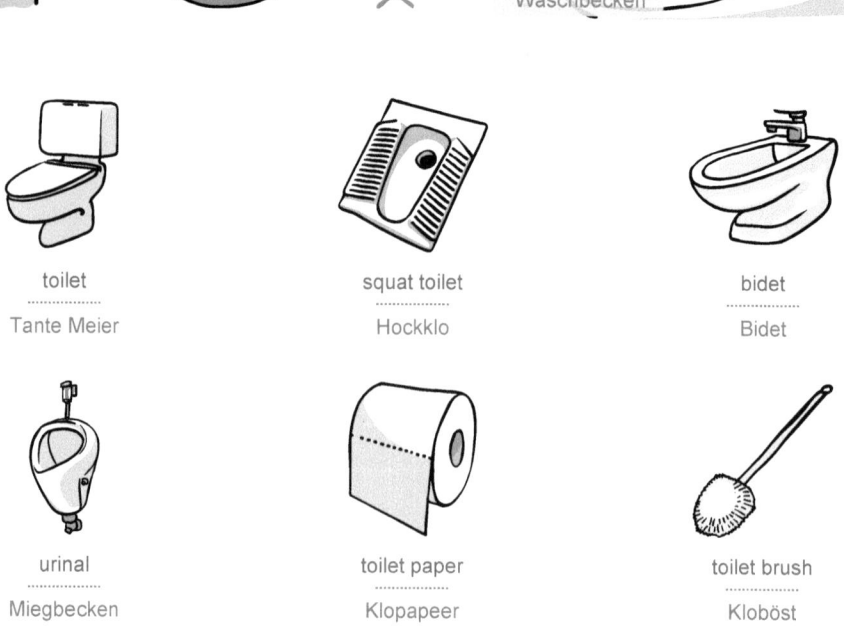

bathroom

Baadstuuv

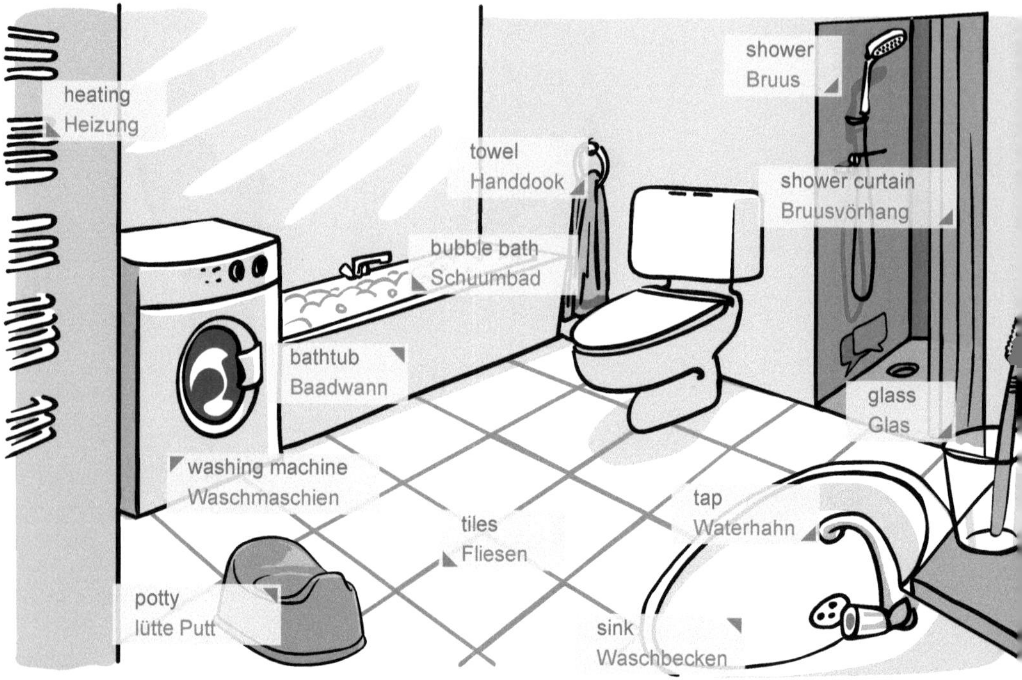

heating
Heizung
towel
Handdook
shower
Bruus
shower curtain
Bruusvörhang
bubble bath
Schuumbad
bathtub
Baadwann
glass
Glas
washing machine
Waschmaschien
tap
Waterhahn
tiles
Fliesen
potty
lütte Putt
sink
Waschbecken

toilet

Tante Meier

squat toilet

Hockklo

bidet

Bidet

urinal

Miegbecken

toilet paper

Klopapeer

toilet brush

Kloböst

toothbrush

Tähnböst

toothpaste

Tähnpast

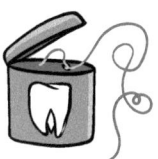

dental floss

Tähnsied

wash

waschen

hand shower

Handbruus

douche

Intimbruus

basin

Waschschöttel

back brush

Rüchböst

soap

Seep

shower gel

Bruusgeel

shampoo

Hoorwaschmiddel

flannel

Waschlappen

drain

Afloop

creme

Creme

deodorant

Deodorant

mirror

Spegel

hand mirror

Kosmetikspegel

razor

Raserer

shaving foam

Raseerschuum

aftershave

Raseerwater

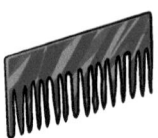

comb

Kamm

brush

Böst

hair-dryer

Hoordröger

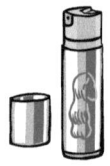

hairspray

Hoorspray

makeup

Smink

lipstick

Lippensticken

nail varnish

Nagellack

cotton wool

Watt

nail scissors

Nagelscheer

perfume

Rüükwater

washbag
Kulturbüdel

stool
Schemel

weighing scales
Waag

bathrobe
Baadmantel

rubber gloves
Gummihanschen

tampon
Tampon

sanitary towel
Damenbinn

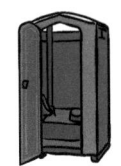

chemical toilet
Chemieklo

kids room
Kinnerstuuv

alarm clock
Wecker
cuddly toy
Knudeldeert
toy car
Speeltüüchauto
rattle
Klöter
doll's house
Poppenhuus
present
Geschenk

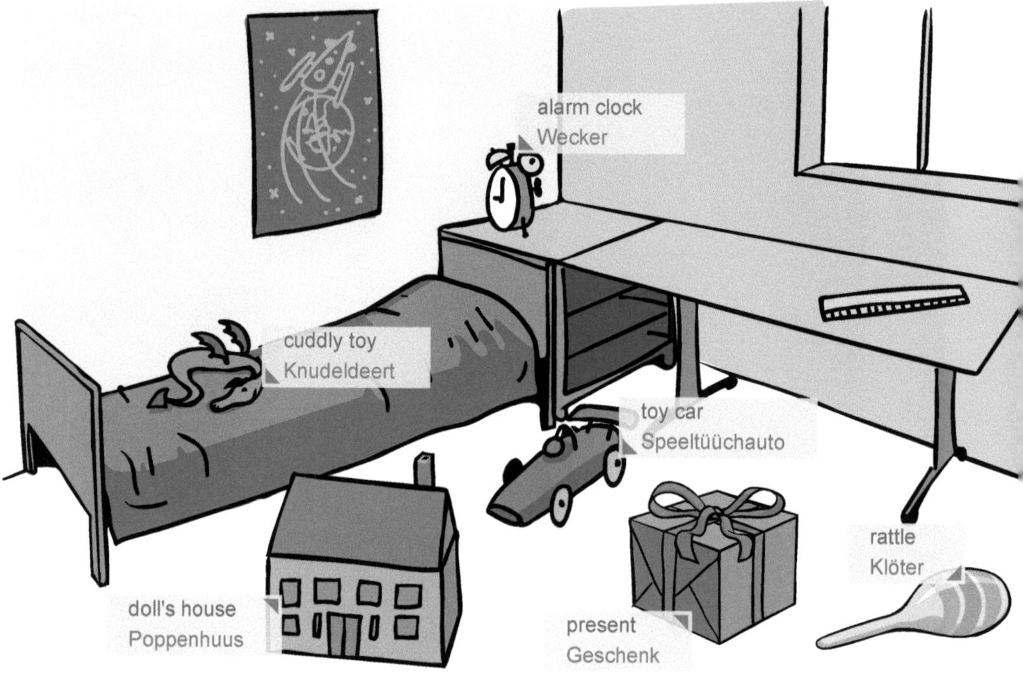

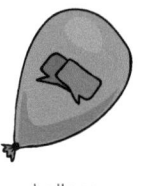

balloon

Luftballon

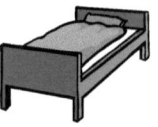

bed

Puuch

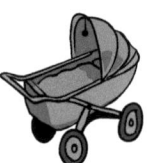

stroller

Kinnerwagen

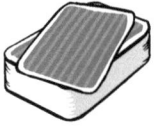

deck of cards

Koortenspeel

jigsaw

Puzzle

SUPER MEGA

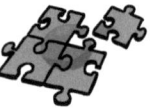

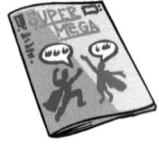

comic

Billergeschicht

lego bricks

Legostenen

toy blocks

Bustenen

action figure

Action-Figur

romper suit

Strampelantog

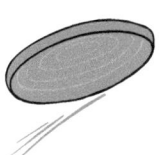

frisbee

Frisbeeschiev

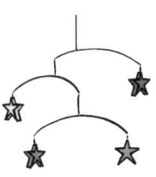

mobile

Mobile

board game

Brettspeel

dice

Wörpel

model train set

Modelliesenbahn

pacifier

Snuller

party

Party

picture book

Billerbook

ball

Ball

doll

Popp

play

spelen

sandpit

Sandkassen

swing

Schuckel

toys

Speeltüüch

video game console

Speelkonsool

tricycle

Dreerad

teddy bear

Teddyboor

wardrobe

Klederschapp

clothing
Tüüch

socks

Socken

stockings

Strümp

tights

Strumpbüx

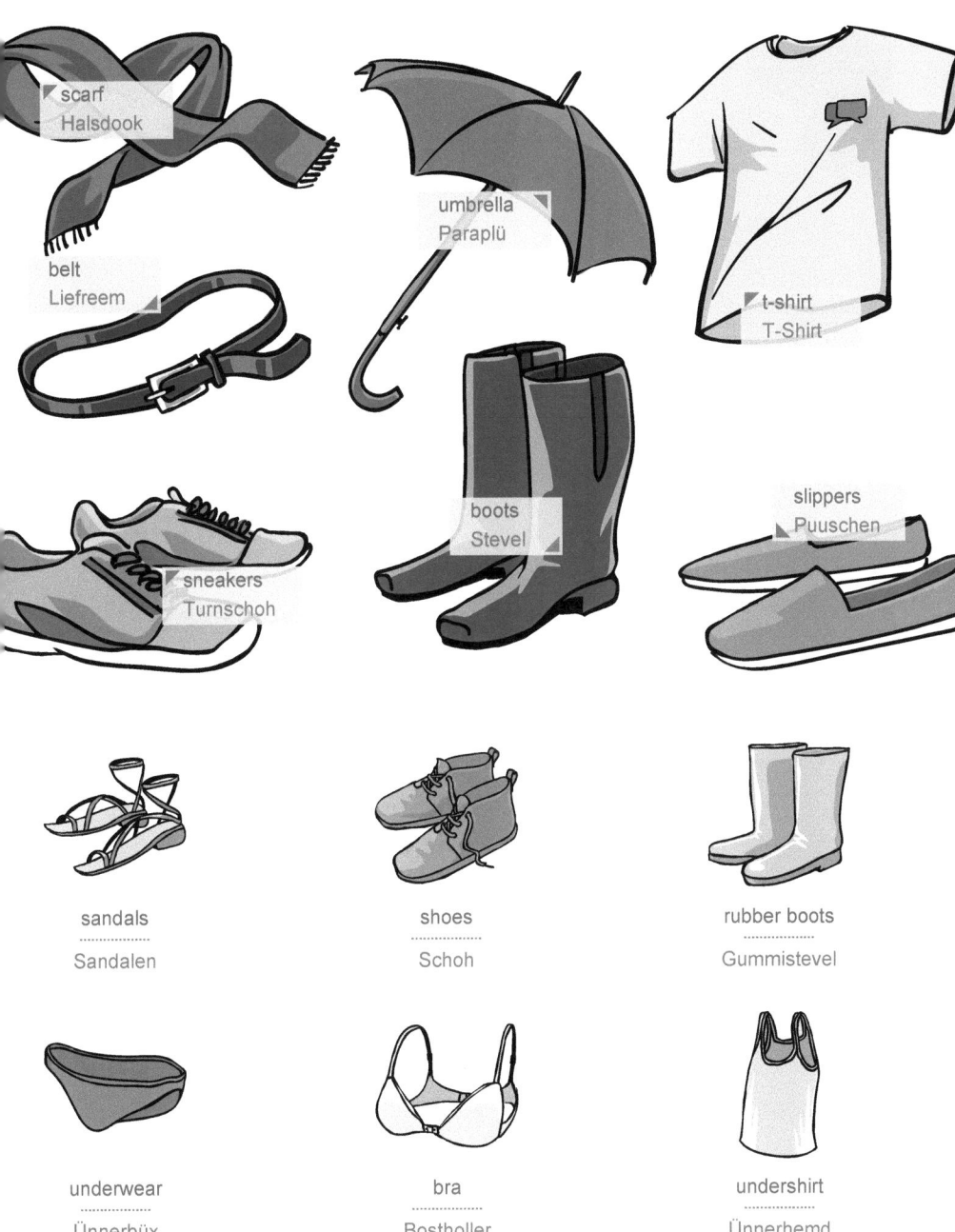

scarf
Halsdook

umbrella
Paraplü

t-shirt
T-Shirt

belt
Liefreem

boots
Stevel

slippers
Puuschen

sneakers
Turnschoh

sandals
Sandalen

shoes
Schoh

rubber boots
Gummistevel

underwear
Ünnerbüx

bra
Bostholler

undershirt
Ünnerhemd

body

Lief

pants

Büx

jeans

Jeansnüx

skirt

Rock

blouse

Bluus

shirt

Hemd

pullover

Pullover

sweater

Kapuzenpullover

blazer

Blazer

jacket

Jack

coat

Mantel

raincoat

Övertrecker

costume

Kostüm

dress

Kleed

wedding dress

Hochtietskleed

suit

Antog

nightgown

Nachtkleed

pajamas

Slaapantog

sari

Sari

headscarf

Koppdook

turban

Turban

burka

Burka

kaftan

Kaftan

abaya

Abaya

swimsuit

Baadantog

trunks

Baadbüx

shorts

Korte Büx

tracksuit

Antog to'n Öven

apron

Schört

gloves

Handschoh

button

Knopp

glasses

Brill

bracelet

Armband

necklace

Halskeed

ring

Ring

earring

Ohrbummel

cap

Mütz

coat hanger

Klederbögel

hat

Hoot

tie

Binner

zip

Rietslüter

helmet

Helm

braces

Drachtband

school uniform

Schooluniform

uniform

Uniform

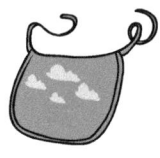

bib

Severböten

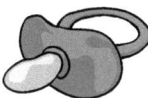

pacifier

Snuller

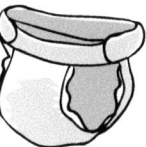

diaper

Winnel

office
Büro

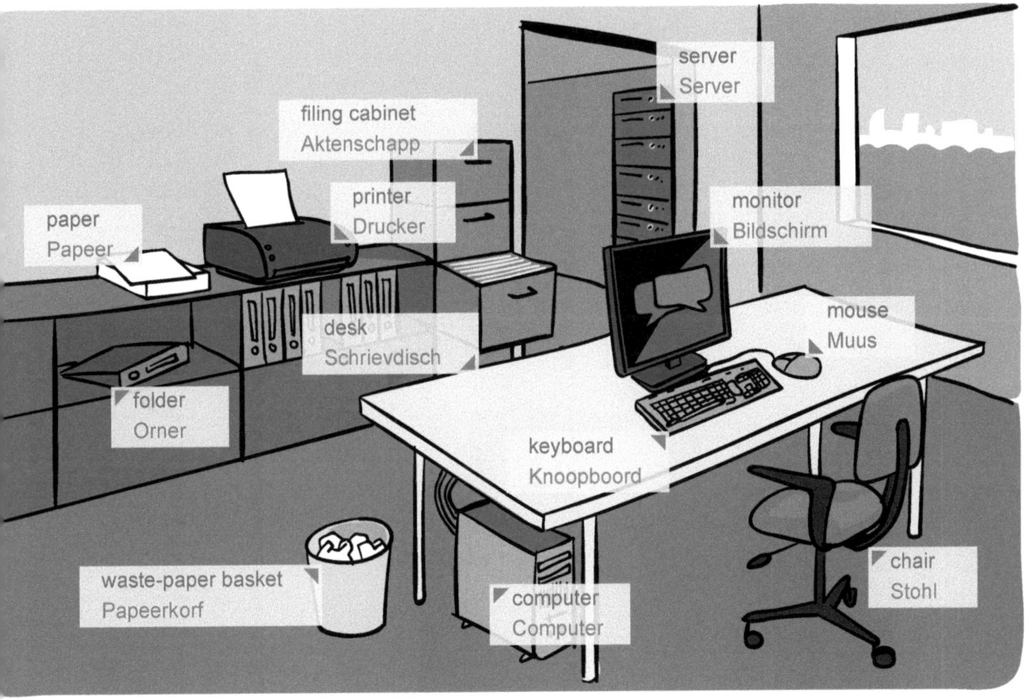
server
Server
filing cabinet
Aktenschapp
printer
Drucker
paper
Papeer
monitor
Bildschirm
mouse
Muus
desk
Schrievdisch
folder
Orner
keyboard
Knoopboord
chair
Stohl
waste-paper basket
Papeerkorf
computer
Computer

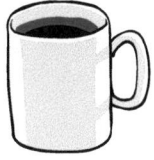

coffee mug

Koffiebeker

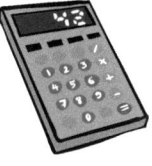

calculator

Taschenreekner

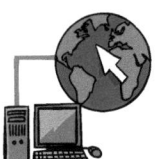

internet

Internet

laptop

Klappreekner

letter

Breef

message

Naricht

cell phone

Ackersnacker

network

Nettwark

photocopier

Kopeerapparat

software

Software

telephone

Klöönkassen

plug socket

Steekdoos

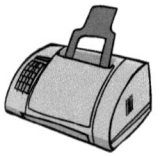

fax machine

Faxapparat

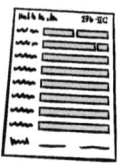

form

Formulor

document

Dokument

office - Büro

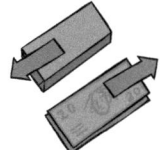

buy

köpen

pay

betahlen

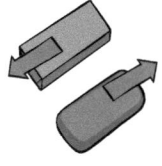

trade

hanneln

money

Geld

 **USD**

dollar

Dollar

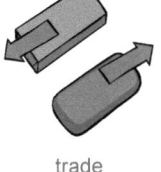 **EUR**

euro

Euro

 **JPY**

yen

Yen

 **RUB**

rouble

Ruvel

 **CHF**

Swiss franc

Swiezer Franken

 **CNY**

renminbi yuan

Renminbi Yuan

 **INR**

rupee

Rupie

cash point

Geldautomat

currency exchange office

Wesselstuuv

gold

Gold

silver

Sülver

oil

Ööl

energy

Energie

price

Pries

contract

Verdrag

tax

Stüer

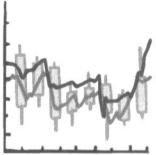

stock

Andeelschien

work

arbeiden

employee

Anstellte

employer

Arbeitgever

factory

Fabrik

shop

Hökerie

occupations
Profeschonen

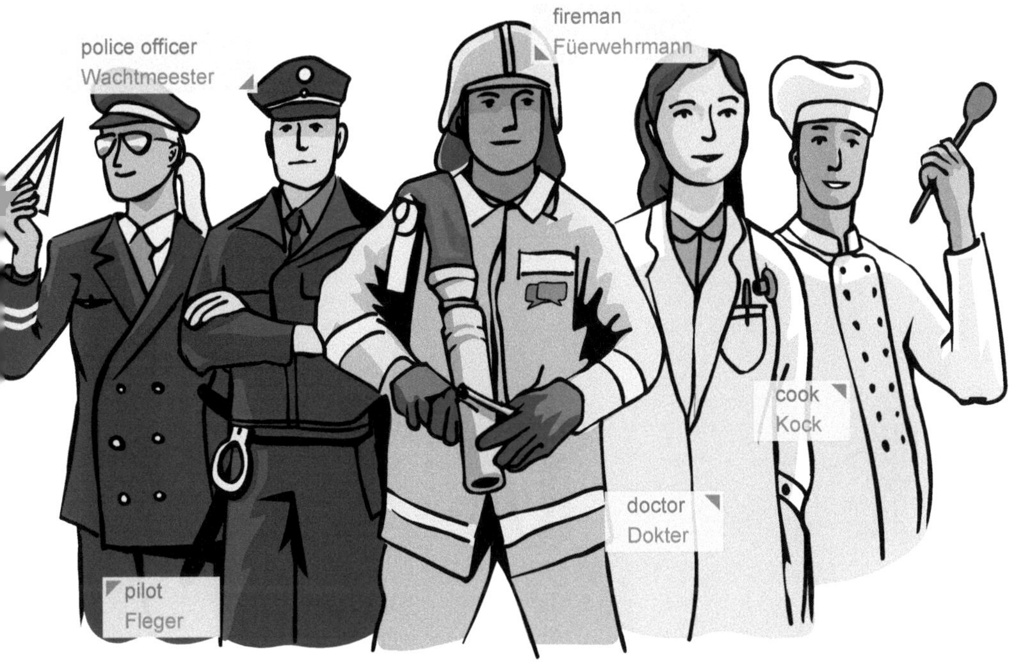
fireman
Füerwehrmann
police officer
Wachtmeester
cook
Kock
doctor
Dokter
pilot
Fleger

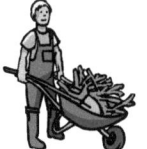

gardener
Goorner

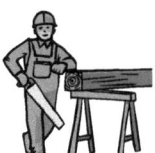

carpenter
Discher

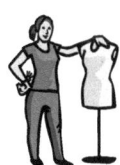

seamstress
Neihersche

judge
Richter

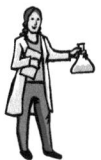

chemist
Chemiker

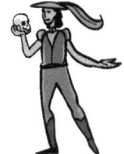

actor
Schauspeler

bus driver

Busfohrer

taxi driver

Taxifohrer

fisherman

Fischer

cleaning lady

Reinmaakfru

roofer

Dackdecker

waiter

Kellner

hunter

Jäger

painter

Maler

baker

Bäcker

electrician

Elektriker

builder

Buarbeider

engineer

Ingenieur

butcher

Slachter

plumber

Klempner

postman

Postbüdel

soldier

Suldat

architect

Architekt

cashier

Kasserer

florist

Florist

hairdresser

Putzbüdel

conductor

Schaffner

mechanic

Mechaniker

captain

Kaptein

dentist

Tähndokter

scientist

Wetenschopler

rabbi

Rabbi

imam

Imam

monk

Mönk

pastor

Paap

tools
Warktüüch

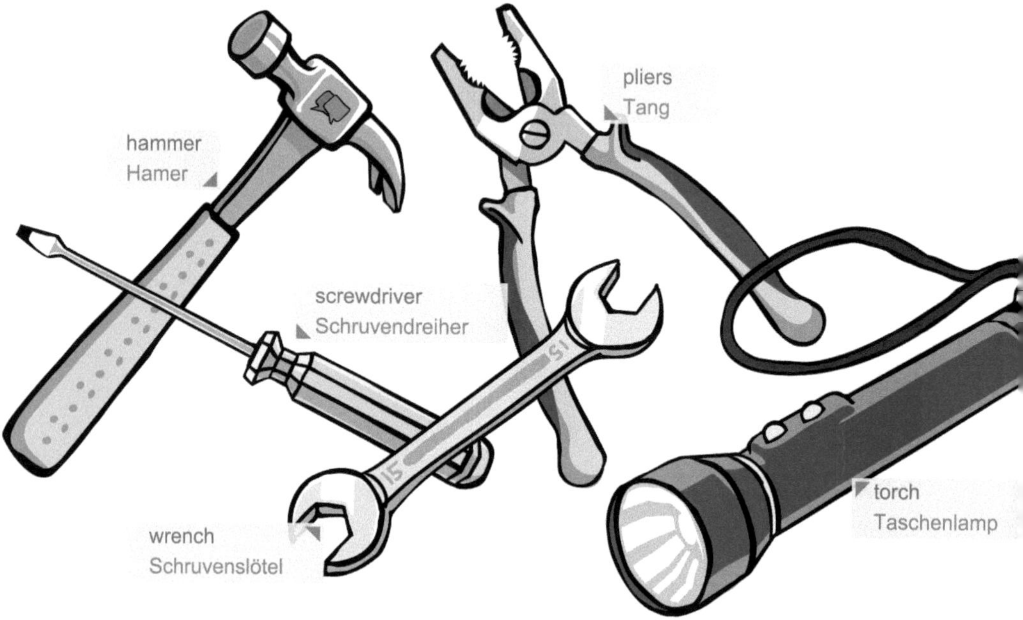

pliers
Tang
hammer
Hamer
screwdriver
Schruvendreiher
wrench
Schruvenslötel
torch
Taschenlamp

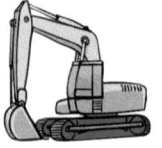

excavator

Grieper

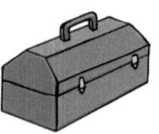

toolbox

Warktüüchkassen

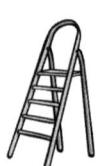

ladder

Ledder

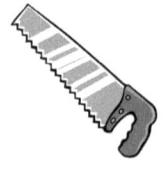

saw

Saag

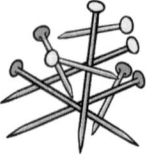

nails

Nagels

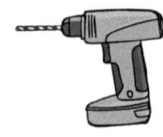

drill

Bohrer

repair

heelmaken

shovel

Schüffel

Damn!

Schiet!

dustpan

Kehrblick

paint can

Farvpott

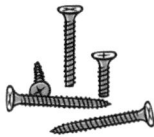

screws

Schruven

musical instruments
Musikinstrumenten

drum set
Slagtüüch

loud speaker
Luutsnacker

guitar
Rietfiedel

double bass
Bass-Vigelien

trumpet
Trumpeet

piano

Klaveer

violin

Vigelien

bass

Bass

timpani

Pauk

drums

Trummeln

keyboard

Keyboard

saxophone

Saxophon

flute

Fleut

microphone

Mikrofoon

zoo
Deertenpark

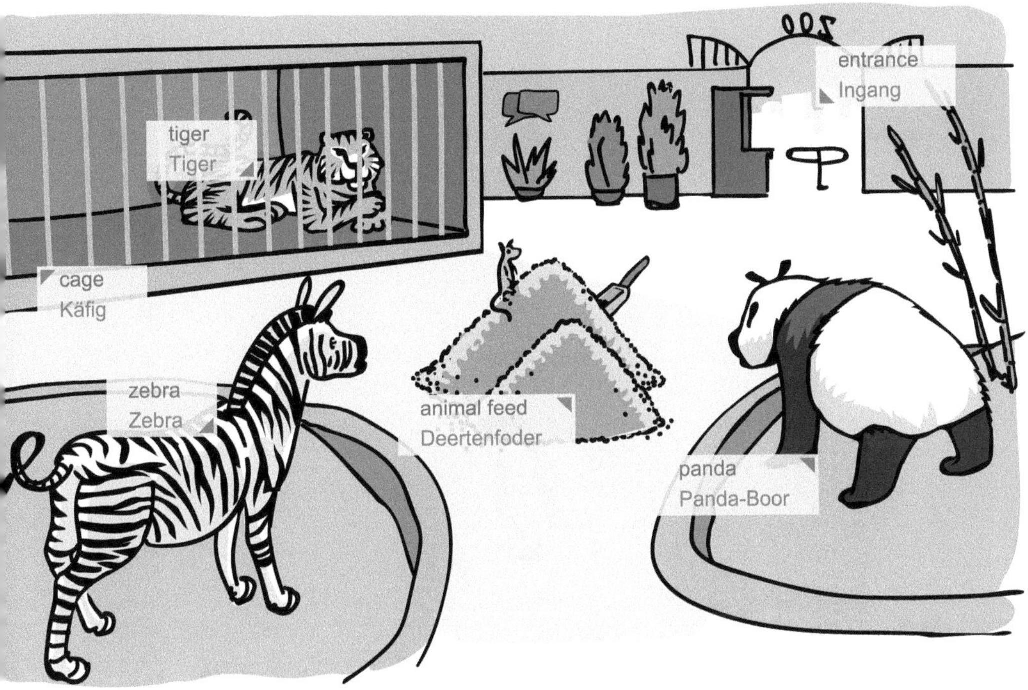
zoo
entrance
Ingang
tiger
Tiger
cage
Käfig
zebra
Zebra
animal feed
Deertenfoder
panda
Panda-Boor

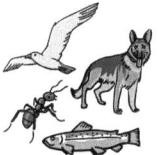

animals

Deerten

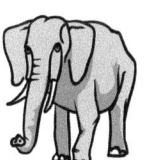

elephant

Elefant

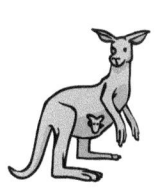

kangaroo

Känguru

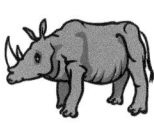

rhino

Neeshoorn

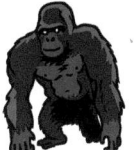

gorilla

Gorilla

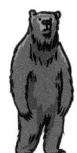

bear

Boor

camel

Kameel

ostrich

Struuß

lion

Lööv

monkey

Aap

flamingo

Flamingo

parrot

Papagoi

polar bear

Iesboor

penguin

Pinguin

shark

Haifisch

peacock

Pageluun

snake

Slang

crocodile

Krokodil

zookeeper

Oppasser in'n Deertenpark

seal

Saalhund

jaguar

Jaguor

pony
Pony

leopard
Leopard

hippo
Nilpeerd

giraffe
Giraff

eagle
Aadler

boar
Wildswien

fish
Fisch

turtle
Schildkrööt

walrus
Walross

fox
Voss

gazelle
Gazell

sports
Sport

American football
Amerikaansch Football

cycling
Radfohren

tennis
Tennis

basketball
Korfball

swimming
Swümmen

boxing
Boxen

ice hockey
Ieshockey

soccer
Football

badminton
Fedderball

athletics
Leichtathletik

handball
Handball

skiing
Skilopen

polo
Polo

jump
springen

laugh
lachen

hug
ümarmen

sing
singen

walk
gahn

dream
drömen

pray
beden

kiss
snuteln

write
schrieven

draw
teken

show
wiesen

push
drücken

give
geven

take
nehmen

have
....
hebben

do
....
doon

be
....
sien

stand
....
stahn

run
....
lopen

pull
....
trecken

throw
....
smieten

fall
....
fallen

lie
....
liggen

wait
....
töven

carry
....
dregen

sit
....
sitten

get dressed
....
antrecken

sleep
....
slapen

wake up
....
opwaken

look at

ankieken

cry

wenen

stroke

eien

comb

kämmen

talk

snacken

understand

verstahn

ask

fragen

listen

hören

drink

drinken

eat

eten

tidy up

oprümen

love

leefhebben

cook

kaken

drive

fohren

fly

flegen

sail

segeln

calculate

reken

read

lesen

learn

lehren

work

arbeiden

marry

de Plünnen tohoopsmieten

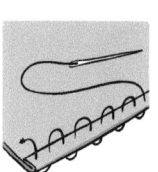

sew

neihen

brush teeth

Tähnen putzen

kill

dootmaken

smoke

smöken

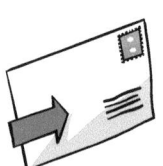

send

schicken

family
Familje

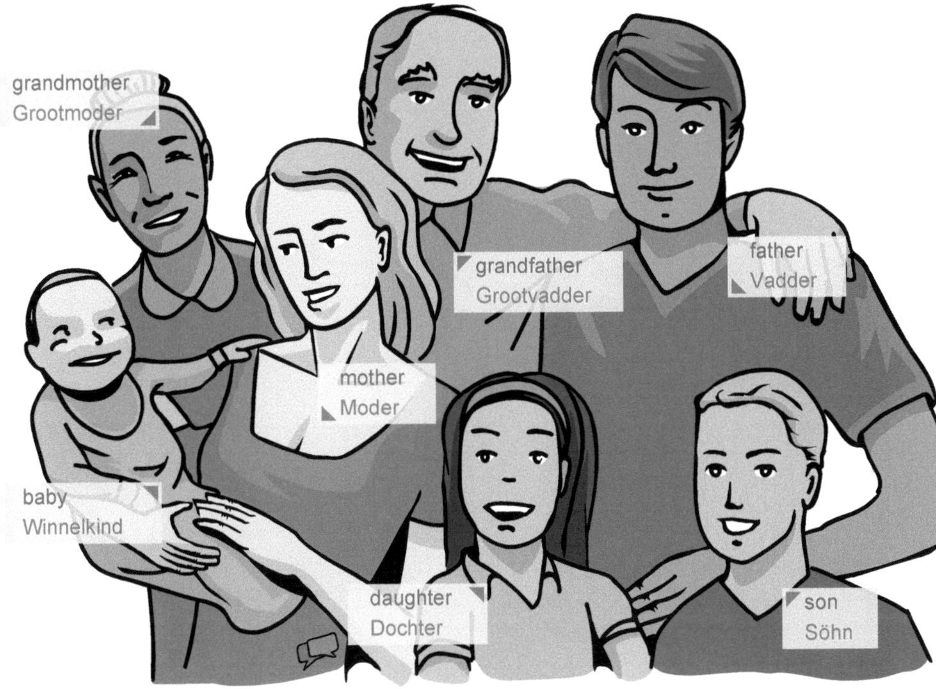
grandmother
Grootmoder
grandfather
Grootvadder
father
Vadder
mother
Moder
baby
Winnelkind
daughter
Dochter
son
Söhn

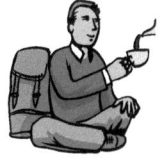

guest
Gast

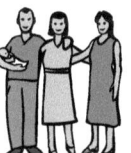

aunt
Tant

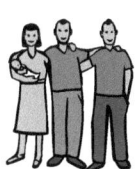

uncle
Unkel

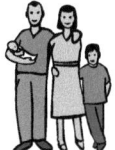

brother
Broder

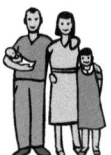

sister
Süster

body
Lief

forehead
Vörkopp
eye
Oog
shoulder
Schuller
finger
Finger
face
Gesicht
chin
Kinn
hand
Hand
leg
Been
breast
Bost
arm
Arm

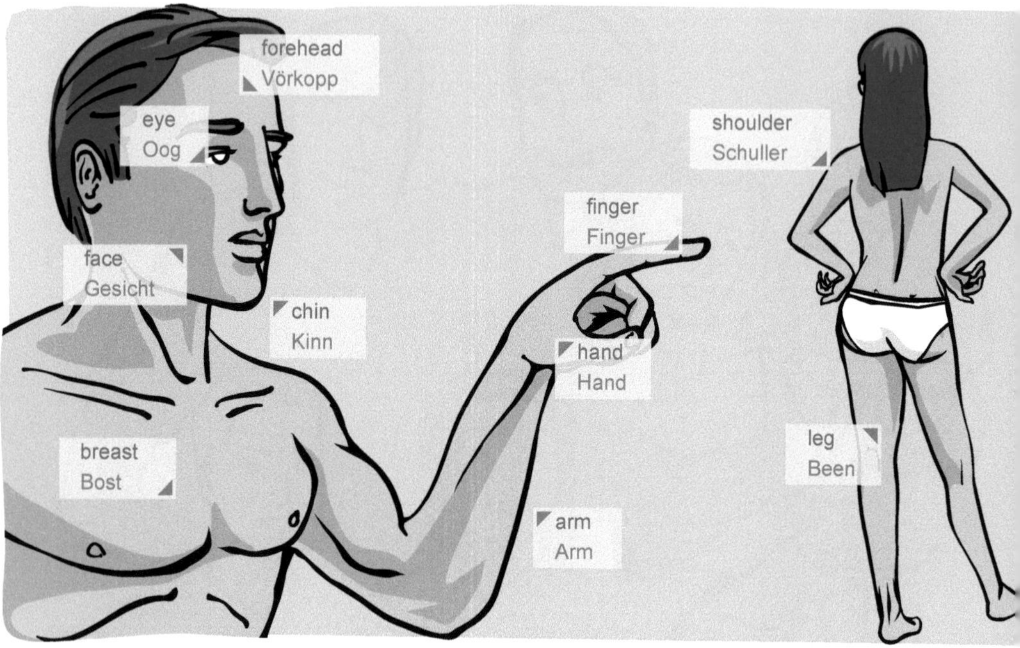

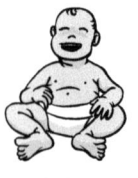

baby

Winnelkind

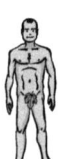

man

Mann

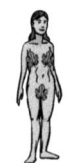

woman

Fro

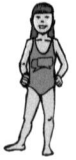

girl

Deern

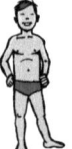

boy

Jung

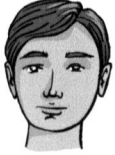

head

Arm

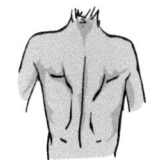

back
Rüch

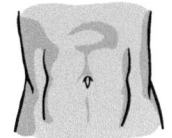

belly
Buuk

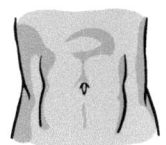

navel
Navel

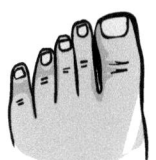

toe
Teh

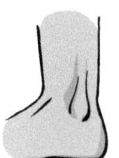

heel
Hack

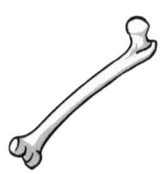

bone
Knaken

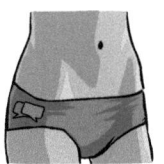

hip
Hüft

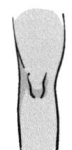

knee
Knee

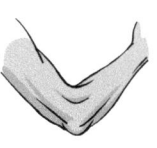

elbow
Ellbagen

nose
Nees

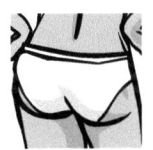

buttocks
Achtersen

skin
Huut

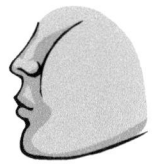

cheek
Back

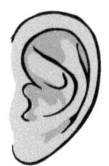

ear
Ohr

lip
Lipp

body - Lief

mouth

Mund

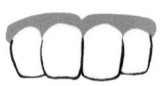

tooth

Tähn

tongue

Tung

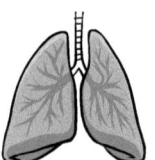

brain

Bregen

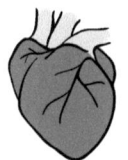

heart

Hart

muscle

Muskel

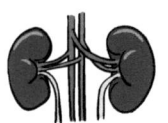

lung

Lung

liver

Lever

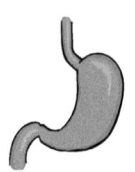

stomach

Maag

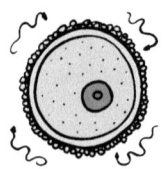

kidneys

Neren

sex

Bislaap

condom

Kondoom

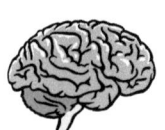

ovum

Eizell

semen

Sperma

pregnancy

Anner Ümstänn

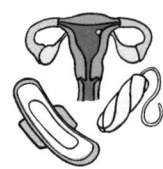

menstruation

Menstruatschoon

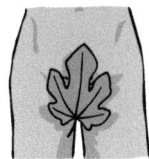

vagina

Scheed

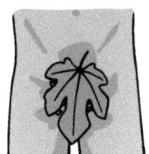

penis

Pint

eyebrow

Ogenbroe

hair

Hoor

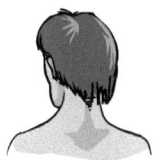

neck

Hals

hospital
Krankenhuus

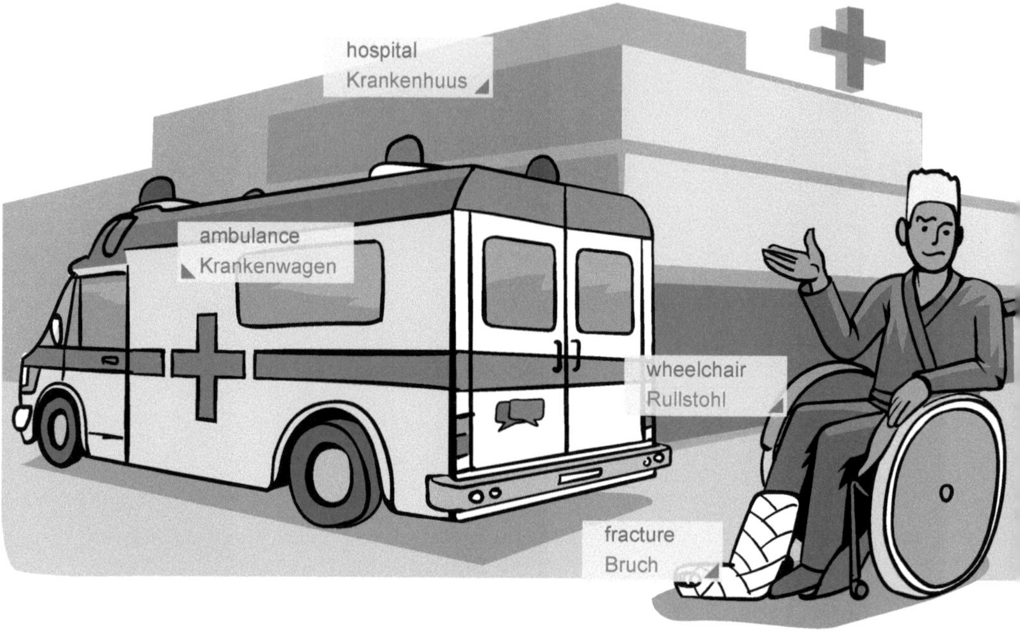

hospital
Krankenhuus
ambulance
Krankenwagen
wheelchair
Rullstohl
fracture
Bruch

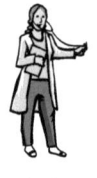

doctor
Dokter

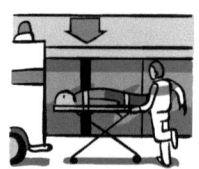

emergency room
Nootopnahm

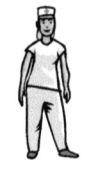

nurse
Krankensüster

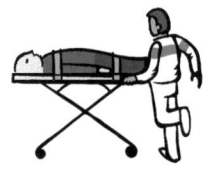

emergency
Nootfall

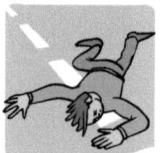

unconscious
ahnmächtig

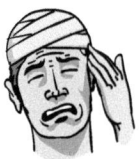

pain
Wehdaag

injury

Verwunnen

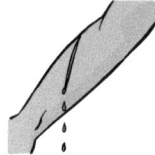

bleeding

Blöden

heart attack

Hartinfarkt

stroke

Slaganfall

allergy

Allergie

cough

Hoosten

fever

Fever

flu

Gripp

diarrhea

Dörchfall

headache

Koppwehdaag

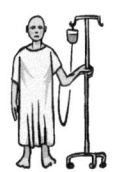

cancer

Kreeft

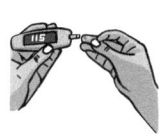

diabetes

Zuckersüük

surgeon

Chirurg

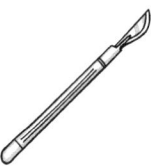

scalpel

Chirurgsch Mess

operation

Operatschoon

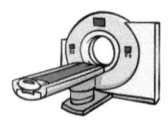

CT

CT

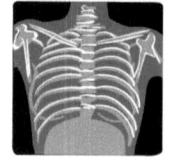

x-ray

Dörchlüchten

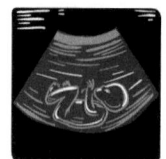

ultrasound

Ultraschall

face mask

Mask

disease

Krankheit

waiting room

Töövruum

crutch

Krück

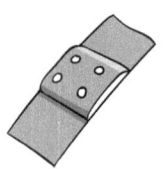

plaster

Plaaster

bandage

Verband

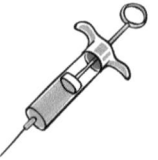

injection

Insprütten

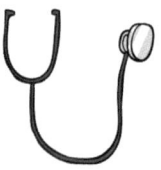

stethoscope

Stethoskop

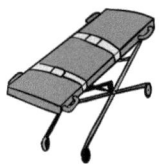

stretcher

Draag

clinical thermometer

Feverthermometer

birth

Geboort

overweight

Övergewicht

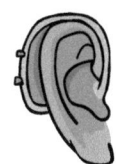

hearing aid

Höörapparat

disinfectant

Kiemfriemiddel

infection

Ansteken

virus

Virus

HIV / AIDS

HIV / AIDS

medicine

Heelmiddel

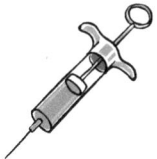

vaccination

Impen

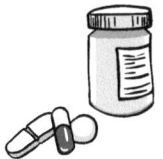

tablets

Tabletten

pill

Pill

emergency call

Nootroop

blood pressure monitor

Blootdruck-Meter

ill / healthy

krank / gesund

Help!	alarm	assault
Hölp!	Alarm	Överfall

attack	danger	emergency exit
Angreep	Gefohr	Nootutgang

Fire!	fire extinguisher	accident
Füer!	Füerlöscher	Unfall

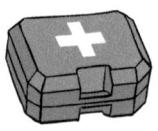		
first-aid kit	SOS	police
Noothölpkoffer	SOS	Polizei

Europe

Europa

North America

Noordamerika

South America

Süüdamerika

Africa

Afrika

Asia

Asien

Australia

Australien

Atlantic

Atlantik

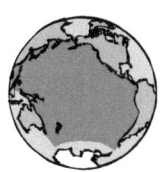

Pacific

Pazifik

Indian Ocean

Indisch Weltmeer

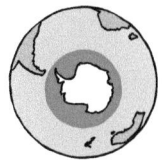

Antarctic Ocean

Antarktisch Weltmeer

Arctic Ocean

Arktisch Weltmeer

North pole

Noordpol

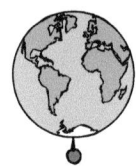

South pole

Süüdpol

Antarctica

Antarktis

earth

Eerd

land

Land

sea

See

island

Eiland

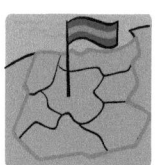

nation

Natschoon

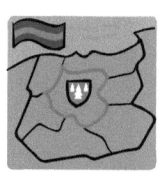

state

Staat

clock face

Tallenblatt

hour hand

Stunnenwieser

minute hand

Minutenwieser

second hand

Sekunnenwieser

What time is it?

Wo laat is dat?

day

Dag

time

Tiet

now

nu

digital watch

digetaalsch Klock

minute

Minuut

hour

Stunn

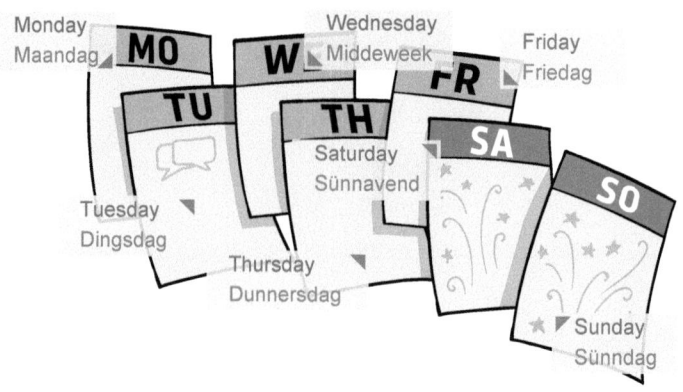

Monday
Maandag — MO

Wednesday
Middeweek

Friday
Friedag

TU

TH

Saturday
Sünnavend

SA

SO

Tuesday
Dingsdag

Thursday
Dunnersdag

Sunday
Sünndag

yesterday
güstern

today
hüüt

tomorrow
morgen

morning
Morgen

noon
Meddag

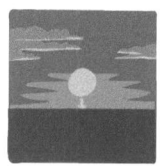

evening
Avend

MO	TU	WE	TH	FR	SA	SU
1	2	3	4	5	6	7
8	9	10	11	12	13	14
15	16	17	18	19	20	21
22	23	24	25	26	27	28
29	30	31	1	2	3	4

workdays
Arbeitsdaag

MO	TU	WE	TH	FR	SA	SU
1	2	3	4	5	6	7
8	9	10	11	12	13	14
15	16	17	18	19	20	21
22	23	24	25	26	27	28
29	30	31	1	2	3	4

weekend
Wekenenn

rain
Regen

snow
Snee

wind
Wind

spring
Fröhjohr

fall
Harvst

summer
Sommer

winter
Winter

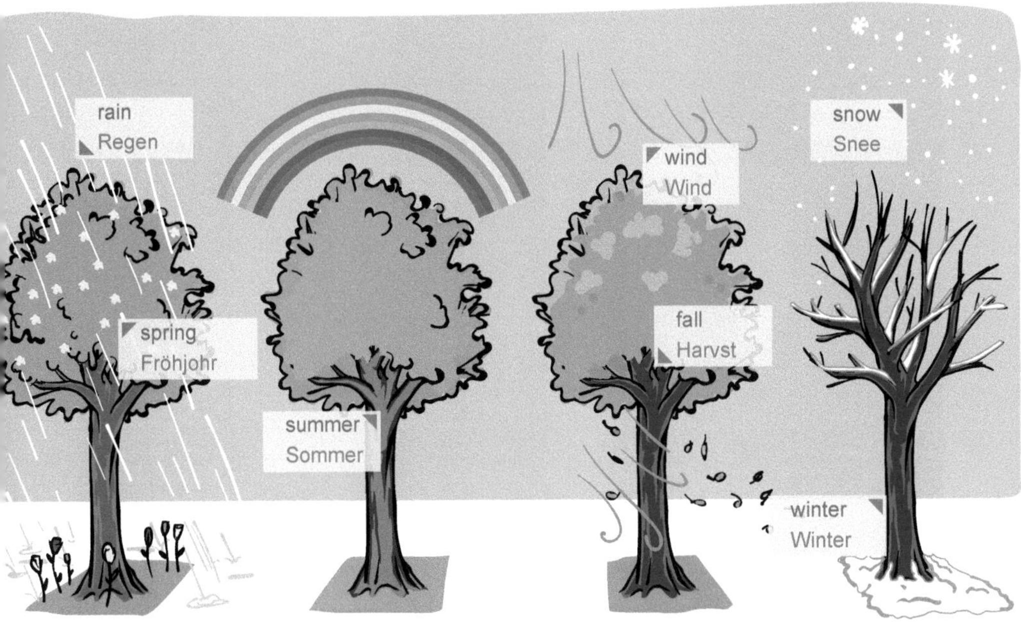

weather forecast
Wedervörhersaag

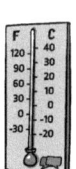

thermometer
Thermometer

sunshine
Sünnenschien

cloud
Wulk

fog
Nevel

humidity
Luftfuchtigkeit

lightning

Blitz

thunder

Dunner

storm

Storm

hail

Hagel

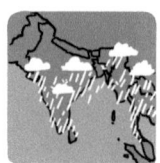

monsoon

Monsun

flood

Floot

ice

Ies

January

Januormaand

February

Februormaand

March

Martmaand

April

Aprilmaand

May

Maimaand

June

Junimaand

July

Julimaand

August

Augustmaand

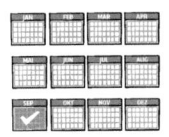

September
Septembermaand

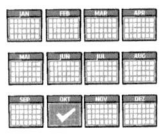

October
Oktobermaand

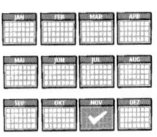

November
Novembermaand

December
Dezembermaand

circle
Krink

square
Quadrat

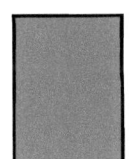

rectangle
Rechteck

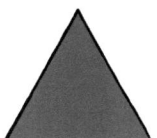

triangle
Dreeeck

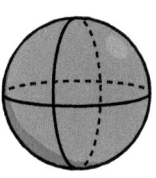

sphere
Kugel

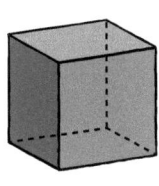

cube
Wörpel

white

witt

yellow

geel

orange

orangsch

pink

pink

red

root

purple

lila

blue

blau

green

gröön

brown

bruun

gray

gries

black

swart

a lot / a little

veel / wenig

angry / calm

böös / verdreeglich

beautiful / ugly

smuck / mies

beginning / end

Begünn / Enn

big / small

groot / lütt

bright / dark

hell / düüster

brother / sister

Broder / Süster

clean / dirty

schier / schietig

complete / incomplete

kumpleet / nich kumpleet

day / night

Dag / Nacht

dead / alive

doot / lebennig

wide / narrow

breet / small

edible / inedible
geneetbor / nich geneetbor

evil / kind
böös / fründlich

excited / bored
fickerig / langwielt

fat / thin
dick / dünn

first / last
toeerst / toletzt

friend / enemy
Fründ / Fiend

full / empty
vull / leddig

hard / soft
hart / week

heavy / light
swoor / licht

hunger / thirst
Smacht / Döst

ill / healthy
krank / gesund

illegal / legal
nich na't Recht / na't Recht

intelligent / stupid
klook / dummerhaftig

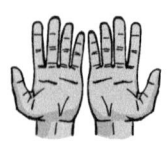

left / right
linkerhand / rechterhand

near / far
neeg / feern

new / used
....
nieg / bruukt

nothing / something
....
nix / wat

old / young
....
oolt / jung

on / off
....
an / ut

open / closed
....
apen / slaten

quiet / loud
....
lies / luut

rich / poor
....
riek / arm

right / wrong
....
richtig / verkehrt

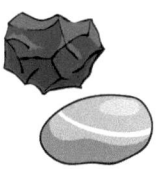

rough / smooth
....
ruug / glatt

sad / happy
....
trurig / glücklich

short / long
....
kort / lang

slow / fast
....
suutje / flink

wet / dry
....
natt / dröög

warm / cool
....
warm / köhl

war / peace
....
Krieg / Freden

0

zero
null

1

one
een

2

two
twee

3

three
dree

4

four
veer

5

five
fief

6

six
söss

7

seven
söven

8

eight
acht

9

nine
negen

10

ten
teihn

11

eleven
ölven

12

twelve

twölf

13

thirteen

dörteihn

14

fourteen

veerteihn

15

fifteen

föffteihn

16

sixteen

sössteihn

17

seventeen

söventeihn

18

eighteen

achtteihn

19

nineteen

negenteihn

20

twenty

twintig

100

hundred

hunnert

1.000

thousand

dusend

1.000.000

million

million

English

Engelsch

American English

Amerikaansch Engelsch

Chinese Mandarin

Chineesch Mandarin

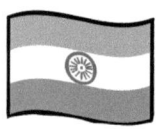

Hindi

Hindi

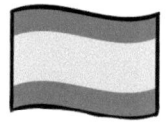

Spanish

Spaansch

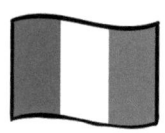

French

Franzöösch

Arabic

Araabsch

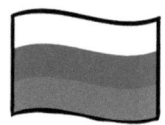

Russian

Rusch

Portuguese

Portugiesch

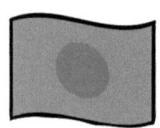

Bengali

Bengaalsch

German

Düütsch

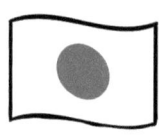

Japanese

Japaansch

I
ik

you
du

he / she / it
he / se / dat

we
wi

you
ji

they
se

who?
keen?

what?
wat?

how?
woans?

where?
woneem?

when?
wannehr?

name
Naam

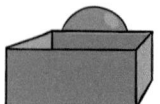

behind

achter

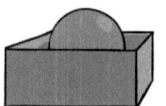

in

in

in front of

vör

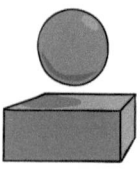

over

över

on

op

under

ünner

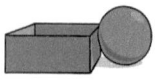

beside

blangen

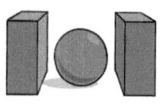

between

twüschen

place

Oort